IMPLICATIONS

BY
CHAN. MCKENZIE

For Mac & John,
Missed friends +
original fans — Hope you like it!

Chan McKenzie

Correspondence/Orders may be sent to:

Sympatico Press
P.O. Box 23822
Rochester, New York 14692

This book was printed by:

Asymmetrical Press
378 Smith Street
Rochester, New York 14608

ISBN 0-9612666-0-0 (pbk.)

Printed in the United States of America

This Book is for Ruby (mom), Patty, and Sherlea. Thank you for the years of support, strength and love.

—*chan.*

TABLE OF CONTENTS

TABLE OF CONTENTS

BROWN

I wish to imply in Brown
a voice which says 'I love me enough
to want . . . from you.'
Brown is pride, it is definition of self,
a proclamation in the endless search for
the right words. Brown bores deep holes in
my sensitive side, where the seeds for my
survival are planted.
Brown poems speak of determination, they
categorize my limitations, in Brown I can
produce concrete statements of who I am
and what I have to offer.

Brown is in essence a poetic roadmap
to my emotional potential,
I write in Brown
to say what lies on my side of the tracks,
it is an enigmatic way of giving out the facts.

OFFERINGS

I know I have smelly sneakers;
Too much hair in the bathroom sink;
and
some pounds you didn't bargain for.

But
If you will see your way
past these few deficiencies,
you will find a love you may have thought
not possible.

The other attributes are workable
maybe.
But the love is
for sure.

THE KIND OF WOMAN

I make amends
        apologies
        consolations
        forgiveness
        rationalizations
        reasons.
I make absolutions
        agreements
        compromise
        concessions
        justifications.
I make excuses
for your behavior
cause I love you
even when you act the fool.
        However,
I in turn expect the same from you
when my shit ain't together.
That's not called demands, honey,
that's just the kind of woman
I am.

A FOREVER

You could say
"Let's get under the sheets
and make hot love
till lunch time."
Or you could say
"Baby, let's take the next train
for Mexico City,
leave it all to just
go on without us."
But dont'cha say
you got something important to do.
Cause honey,
when you talk like that,
you make me feel
like a weekend
instead of
a forever.

BRONX KIDS

Bronx kids
do not acquire grace
easily.

Honey
dontcha compre̒nde?

I have
rough edges - sure
but
they were made
from years of being
not enough
of tough.

These enemy forces
are rough
indeed
but
my center,
she, is velvet.

A WRITER

I want to be
a writer
so
when I tell you off Honeee
the Lord
and Chicago
will know about it.

I want to be
a writer
so
when I say I love you Honeee
Kansas City
and my mama
will call to say
I heard that!

ANOTHER DESIRE

If you want me
to tell you
it's okay
to go and be
with someone else,
I suggest
you best-ta
get yourself
another desire.

CROSS-TA-BEAR

I don't want to
talk about yourself tonight,
cause I'm afraid
I may upset mah-self.
But as long as we are
on the subject this evening
you really should know
I been asking mah-self,
"Where is that damn fool tonight?"
Lord knows
why,
but
I'm afraid
that loving you
must be mah
cross-ta-bear

COOL

Yes I'm cool
no response
dig me
no unnecessary emotions displayed.

Yes I can handle it
I am cool, remember?
I can deal.

NO!
d-don't tell me anymore
I-I do not wish
to hear it said, confessed.
It is done.
I understand - a
thing that happened.

Yes, I see.
Well, uh, it looks like rain out there.
No, no, really.
I'm fine
I'm sure
yes
I
I am cool.

KID LOOSE

Wait
till the wild ones hear!
Kid Loose
is out again.
One of their own
has returned.
I will tell everyone
that you are back on your own.
The stores will close,
bands will play,
confetti will fall - - and I will
sweep you out my back door
and slam it.
I-will-let-you-go-to-your-cheering-crowds
all those nameless, adoring faces
I will let you have your bright night lights
        let you hum your secret love songs.
I will sweep and be happy.
Wait
till the world knows
Kid Loose is swinging-single again.
Won't the good Lord be glad to hear
that you have taken your devil-may-care
and finally left this
poor tired girl alone.

... AND TIRED

I have been teacher
       lover
       friend
I have been thrown out
       shared
       let in
I have been mine
       yours
       undecided
I am now
all of the above,
and tired.

BLUE

I don't know what it is
I only know that it is hanging
all around me.
Something is not right, something
no longer feels like it should,
the good is gone,
These are Blues.

I find Blue poems without having to search
for sultry subject matter. Blue poetry writes
itself, I am only there to guide the pen.

The circumstances which evoke Blue are
often those for which no appropriate words
were opportunely exchanged. These could
also be called leftover phrases, for they
are fragments of the moment, hours later.
To write Blue, it is necessary to purge these
pent up emotions.

Although at times a subtle humor can be found
in the expressions of Blue, in truth Blues are
an anchor in the sadness of most situations. Or as
I have found, a poetic means of laughter to
keep from crying.

TWO BEATS

My heart skipped two beats
when I heard you'd moved
left town
and no forwarding address
Though maintaining my composure
I could feel my smile
fade to despair
as I realized
we had grown so far apart
that I was no longer considered
among your good-byes

ONE TIME, HARD

I would not have believed
it could be like this
and even now
I refuse to recognize the changes
you put me through.
Lord knows
I was happy as hell
before you walked in
and stuck a spoon full of you
up my nose.
There just ain't no way
I would have believed loosing you
would mean
spending time on my belly
with my ass in the air . . .
If you would have just kicked me
one time, HARD
right before you took your leave
I'm sure it would have been better
than spending time in this hell
singing the loosing you blues
with tears in my eyes.

COME GET THEM

There are some principle doubts
         some nagging, unanswered questions.
There are some bad feelings
     and a certain amount of anger.
There are tears.
There is rage,
and there is still the bitch in me
        to contend with.

Yes,
I do believe
you may have left a few things behind.

Come get them.

THANKS

These dark days
full of suspicion
which you have given me . . .
Thanks.
Now, instead of
feeling much too secure
I am having
doubts
having
anger,
having
suspicions . . .
Thanks.
Somehow it does not
soothe to know how much
I've given to make this love
secure,
while in return
I find myself
with dark days
full of suspicion.
Thanks.

TRUE CONFESSIONS

Yeah.
And sometimes
when it rains I
shut off all my lights,
sit on my bed and pray
lightning won't strike my house.
And
there is truth
to that crazy rumor
which claims I can be terrorized
by a mouse no bigger than
my big toe.
And
once in awhile
I do worry about
where you've been,
when you'll come back,
and
why I get queasy feelings
whenever you've been gone too long.

4 DAMN THIRTY

I hope that you were not expecting
a rousing round of Bill Bailey wontcha
or a short rendition of Armstrong's Dolly
or a few bars by the Preservation Hall Jazz Band
or nothin.
After all, it is
4:30 in the morning
and I was bound to
get tired of waiting
and nod.
However,
that does not at all
answer the original question:
What do people like you do
till
FOUR
DAMN
THIRTY??

WITHOUT THE SUN

Yesterday,
as we were walking to the Mill
talking casually about
what should have been 'true confessions'
for both of us; but instead turned out to be
you ripping the sun out of my life
and the breath from my soul.

Not knowing what you were saying
you have always said just enough (of nothing really)
to make me keep on trying . . .

Yesterday,
when you finally did say something
you tore me apart
even though I managed to keep on walking,
smiling and trying to be convincing as I said
I was "really happy and everything for ya."

But I really hate her guts I think
and wish that you had remained silent and said
nothing at all really, like you'd done before . . .

Cause,
I didn't need to go shopping anyway
and I sure didn't need to have my heart torn up.

PRECAUTIONS

I bout' near choked
when I heard you'd be in town this weekend
I cancelled all my plans
and boarded up my house.
I refuse to budge
for the next two days
for fear I might
run into you somewhere
and find out
I still love you.

PREDICATE

There is a chilly breeze
between us.

We are two plateaus
with a great gorge
dividing.
Seperate
Singular
Silent
You lie deep within yourself
I am already becoming my own
protective enclosure.
Day
after
day, we are . . . drifting.

This place is cold.
I shudder.

HAD-BAD

I declare
I swear
I dear-dear me
I think
I've just
been took.
I fear
I can't bear
to believe
I was hooked
by the look
in your eyes.

This makes me humble
makes me regret
every chance
I've ever taken
and Lord, let's not mention
all the sacrifices I've made.

Oo
Oo
EE
I be had,
bad.

PURPLE

Purple is a color which defies deference.
When I tell what I want or
when I say what I feel
poetically it is Purple.
This voice makes perceptively precise statements.
It comes from strong overwhelming feelings or
preferences. Purple poems can be so bold, that
there is a tendency toward making resolute
pronouncements which cannot later be disavowed.
Purple poetry is not intentionally written to
be so explicit,
it cannot be avoided.
Poetry is always passionately compelled.

YOU DO

Finally
instead of, "I want some who- -"
does this
like so and so,
or
likes that
like whatsaname usta,
or
has a cute face
like
you know who.
Finally
I can say, "I want someone who- -"
do what you do
when you do it
how you do it.
You do it
Like I've been all the time
hoping and praying
I could find me a somebody
who would be doing it
like you.

BACK TO WOLF MEAT

Back to wolf meat
the cold again familiar.
Wet barstools,
frigid friendships,
nights made of rough concessions.
Back to wolf meat,
let loose and on my own.
     Oh, but it gets hard
     living on the fringes.
     Sometimes I could use
     a little of your generous reprieve.
     I have need for
     strong solace,
     familiar fingers,
     two or three months of
     same old same.
My body is stranded here in
single city,
tired of callous, casual contacts
with no way to
change your mind so
I can go back to where
I once was blindly fulfilled.

. . . THEN WHAT?

I may go to bed with you
hug you and kiss you
tell you all my thoughts
that float by at the present moments.

I may hold you close to me
feel myself becoming a part of you
vow to always want you.

I may say things
that I have not said before.
I may moan and sigh
as though I would never
and have never
felt the way I feel with you.

I may want you, and please you
but if I do not love you - -
then what?

IN THE LAND OF SOMETIMES

it's cold out there in the land of
sometimes, just north of maybe
around the corner in a bar
i'm not always sure
that being single
is the same as being alone
or
for that matter
being married
is akin to being tied down
i guess
all i know at this point
is that it's cold out there
where i am free to not love anyone
and warm as an afrikan jungle
inside this thing i have with you

THE THINGS WE SAY AT NIGHT

The things we say at night
are such things
as lovers have been known to say.
Familiar refrains,
solitary statements,
clarifications,
a compromise with honor.
I am,
laying down my battle weapons
at your feet,
laying down my no's and never's
for you to store away
in such a gentle place as your heart.

The things we say at night,
in dark surrender,
clinging to a certain touch.
Independent needs,
justifiable hesitations,
decisions,
a peace treaty of sorts.
I am baring down my walls
for the want of you,
baring down my soul
for you to place within your tenderness
cradling it like a child to your breast.

PASSING FANCY

If ya think
this is just a
passing fancy baby,
then I dare you
to try
and walk away.

WELCOME MAT

I don't need
someone
who will say alot of nothing.

I don't need
no one
who will try
to change my style.

I don't need
anyone
who will hang over me,
playing owner.

But,
I do need a babee
who will love me like crazy.
Back and forth
up and down
round and round.
Tender, gentle and with
real emotion.

Now,
if that's what you have in mind,
you can come in.

ON MONOGAMY

I don't really care
what you do
just so long as
you remember
I love you more than anything.
And if I ever lose you,
I'll be alone in the world.
You are free to make
your own decision.
You have to do what's best for you.
I won't stand in your way,
cause it's no good
if you do it only
because I want you to
So
go on, think it through
and whatever you decide
is fine with me
as long as I don't
ever find out what you did.

P.S.

thanks for writing me to say
politely
you are fine,
and still in love.
Did you ever really understand what I said
that night we had steaks and wine?
How strange it seems now
to remember categorizing my adorations
so as not to scare you away.
I know now that I tread so
softly
into your affections
that you mistook it
for indifference.
I will not open musty closet doors
by sending desperate prose
through the mail.

I will simply say
the weather is fine; and I
no longer believe in fairies.

OTHER WOMEN

There will always be
other women
who come and go,
leaving as I enter,
staying behind
when I go home.
There will always be
nights without you,
and days when I am not
so sure anymore that I
can take it all in stride.
So, I will remember
the woman that I was before you,
one who slept satisfied with
partial surrender.
I was living on the edge of
feeling for real.
There will always be
other women - -
before me, instead of me.
But, I intend to be there
when all is said and done.

RED

When my toes curl
When my socks rock
When my liver quivers
I've got Red material.

Red beats hard like a bass drum
and is in itself an implication of
syncopation.

When I feel dangerous
When I court seduction
When I see possibilities
Red poems come pouring out.

Red can be hot and they can be bold
Red poems are not respectable and they
don't care.

Red demands attention
it flirts for it
it hurts for it
Red poems do not know
how to behave.
It is only recently that I have
been able to write RED
it was because I was too young to
understand the rhythmn of Red.
Now that I am older I
have a need to testify.

FROM ONE PLAYER, TO ANOTHER

Honey,
take your one night stand,
     your blaise aires,
     your seductive smile,
     that open-necked shirt, . . .
     and all those other lovers
        that you've been hinting about
        for the last three hours - -
Put them in this bag, . . .
and follow me into the next room.
If there's anything else
that need be said,
we can talk about it
in the morning.

EGO TRIPPING

I intend

to pull your feet out

from under your legs,

then

boldly jump before you,

to catch

as you fall down

hard

into my loving.

MY HEAD DOWN, STEADY

i want to feel you
warm on my mouth
as you clutch a pillow in one hand
and my head down steady
in the other,
pushing my tongue
closer against your loving
as you climb towards the ceiling,
passionately calling my name.

69

loving inside circles,
with a blues beat
tapping our feet
to the steady sound
of going down easy
on each other slowly
to the core
of what a feeling is
I am taking from you
the juices of your sweet love,
and giving in return,
my own.

AMAZON LOVE SONG

I take the nights
    like a desert rat
    desperately gulps cool puddles of water
  the hours
    grabbing the hands of time
    to keep them from moving so quickly
  the moments
    greedily stuffing them inside me
    for sustanance between our times.
I take you smiles
    my eyes like Nikkons
    capturing each of your expressions
  your touches
    innocently wanting more,
    while trying to ignore the few
  your mouth
    trying hard not to go crazy on you.
I take the nights
    the ones you give me
I take the days
    the ones you save me
I take the drops of water on my brow
    to quell the flame,
    calm the fire,
    cool the fever.

SYMPATICO

I
am going to write
"TA-DA's!"
about
how it feels
to wake up in the morning
and see you
lying there
with your shoulders
exposed.

REACTIONS

When you kissed me
I felt
my body
s
l
i
d
e to the floor,
      and then quickly
      bounce up
      seeking more.

I went down

I got
clipped.
Right at the
knee bone
I got
hit
hard and my
legs buckled under.
I got knocked
d
o
w
n . . . and I was l
       a
        yed flat.
I got loved chile,
and I stayed
down for the C-O-U-N-T.

TREAT THE BEAT

Knowing
that you will
treat the beat
so gently,
waiting is
a couple of warm,
fluid sighs,
followed by moments
of desperately steady
anticipation.

WHEN YOU GET HERE

I want you
to come back
so badly,
that I
don't care
if you say
you didn't miss me,
when you get here.